SEVEN MIRACLES
IN
VIETNAM

Signed By: Tuesday 1-3-2017

Paul W. Simmons

PAUL W. SIMMONS

To: Susan

VALOR ENTERPRISES

ESCONDIDO, CALIFORNIA

Valor Enterprises
955 Howard Avenue, Spc. #31
Escondido, CA 92029
Phone +1 (760) 705-5391
simmonstrek28@outlook.com

Publishing Manager: Helen Chang, www.authorbridgemedia.com
Editor: Kristine Serio, www.authorbridgemedia.com
Original Book Cover Designer: Marco A. Williams
Book Cover Designer: Laura Duffy

Library of Congress Control Number: 2015910851
ISBN 978-1-943778-00-3 Paperback
ISBN 978-1-943778-01-0 Ebook

Ordering Information:
Quantity sales: Special discounts are available on quantity purchases by
corporations, associations, and others. For details, contact the publisher
at the address above.

Printed in the United States of America

THIS BOOK IS DEDICATED TO YOU,
THE READER.

I hope you are
inspired by the seven miracles
written in these pages.

May God bless you.

Acknowledgments

I thank God, Jesus Christ, and the Holy Ghost for these seven miracles, and for saving my life and the lives of everyone in my unit while I was in Vietnam.

I am also thankful for the prayers of support from my wife and family, before, during, and after returning to the United States from Vietnam. I'm grateful for my wife of more than twenty-one years, Alicia, for helping me with this book. My parents, Fred Groves (1925–1986) and Maxine Groves (1926–2012), raised me, and I am thankful to them. I thank my sisters, Bonnie, Pam, and Debbie, and in particular my brother, Jim, for being close to me and sharing everything with me growing up.

I am grateful to Marco A. Williams for creating the book cover design.

To Helen Chang and Kristine Serio at Author Bridge Media, I thank both of you for helping me with this book. I could not have written it without you.

Finally, I thank all of my units—1st BN/40th Artillery, Charley Battery, 108th Group; and 1st BN/44th Artillery, Bravo Battery—for their teamwork in keeping each other alive. My heart goes out to all the Vietnam soldiers who did not make it home. I think about those soldiers every day, as a memorial to their memories.

Contents

THE HEART OF GOD

Romans 10:9 reads, "If you confess with your mouth the Lord Jesus, and believe in your heart that God has raised him from the dead, you will be saved."

I lived out the truth of that Bible verse. For thirteen months between August 1969 and September 1970, I served in the Vietnam War as a soldier in the United States Army. Those thirteen months were the most devastating days of my life.

And yet, in the middle of unspeakable horror, I witnessed God perform miracles.

The power of faith can never be fully captured in words. Faith can save us from the impossible. In times of helplessness, it provides help. In times of hopelessness, it restores hope. When we are frustrated, it lends us the strength to overcome our challenges. When we are joyful, it gives us a heightened appreciation of our blessings.

In times of fear, faith surprises us. And in times when we can see no path forward, faith makes a way.

My goal with this book is not to force anyone to believe the way I do. What you want to believe is entirely up to you. My faith is rooted in my own experiences, including the seven miracles I'm about to share in these pages. Your faith is something that comes from you.

This world we live in seems to grow bleaker every day. But in spite of the sorrow and the wars, I truly believe that we can have heaven on earth within ourselves. We need only ask for the wisdom and understanding to create it. When we do, the Lord gives it to us freely.

During my thirteen months in Vietnam, I carried my Bible with me everywhere I went. It gave me the faith I needed to believe that God would bring me back from the war alive. Even in the face of death, I believed that God would save me, and He did—more than seven times. My parents, grandparents, and siblings prayed for me and for all of us soldiers every day that I was there.

I give God all the credit for my survival, and to this day I thank him for saving my life and the lives of everyone in my unit.

Everything written in these pages is true. The seven miracles you're about to read happened to me exactly as they unfold in these chapters. I hope you will be inspired by them.

May these seven miracles edify God and serve as a blessing to you, the reader. May your heart open fully to the power of faith.

May you believe in miracles.

1/44TH ARTILLERY BRAVO BATTERY

Town in Quang Tri Province.

April 1970

Chapter 1

THE ROOT OF FAITH

*Whoever calls on the name of
the Lord shall be saved.*

—ROMANS 10:13

When I was seven years old, my grandmother witnessed me for Christ.

It happened around ten o'clock on a warm, sunny morning in Compton, California. I had stayed over with my grandparents the night before, as I did sometimes. My grandfather was off doing something in another room. My grandmother Grace and I were alone in her light-filled sitting room, sitting on the sofa together. She had the Bible in her lap.

My grandmother often read the Bible with me. Sometimes we read the Old Testament—David killing Goliath to save Israel, Moses parting the Red Sea.

I loved those stories with the faith and amazement of a child.

That morning, we were going to read another one. I had just finished breakfast. The house smelled faintly of fresh meatloaf—my favorite dish—from the night before. I sat next to my grandmother on the sofa and waited for her to open the Bible.

Instead, she looked at me with her kind, knowledgeable brown eyes and asked, "Paul, would you like to be saved?"

I was surprised, but I was also excited. I was ready. I wanted to know God. "Yes, I would, Grandma," I answered. "Should I get on my knees?"

"Yes, go ahead. Get on your knees," she nodded. I knelt on her light gray carpet. My grandmother folded her hands in prayer. "Now repeat after me," she began.

I echoed her words as she recited a version of Romans 10:9. "If you confess with your mouth to the Lord Jesus, and believe in your heart that God has raised him from the dead, you will be saved."

"Would you like to receive Jesus Christ into your heart?" she asked.

I answered, "Yes, I would."

"Do you believe that you are saved now that you have accepted Jesus Christ into your heart?" she went on.

"Yes," I replied, "I do believe I am saved."

Then she said, "Would you like to receive the Holy Spirit right now?"

I said that I would. And as I spoke those words, a feeling of warmth came over my heart. I felt the presence of the Holy Ghost filling me with unspeakable joy for the first time. Tears of happiness filled my eyes and ran down my cheeks. An unknown language rose in me, and I began to speak without understanding what I was saying. I didn't need to know.

The Holy Spirit was speaking to God through me.

Several minutes went by, and then the words stopped. A feeling of calm came over me. I got up from my knees and sat beside my grandmother on the couch again.

She didn't say anything. Nothing needed to be said. She just looked at me with her brown eyes and smiled. I smiled back at her.

Then she opened the Bible in her lap and began to read.

* * *

Religion remained a very important part of my life while I was growing up. Long before I got to Vietnam, I saw my share of miracles.

In third grade, I was playing in the sandbox with the other children when I looked up and saw Jesus Christ standing on a cloud. It had rained not too long ago. The clouds were big, fluffy, and white, and the sun was shining through them. Jesus stood on one in a glorified body, his hands held out to me. He had blue eyes, and he wore a white robe. He was smiling.

I watched him for a moment, filled with excitement. Then I turned to tell the other children, "Hey look, it's Jesus up there in the cloud!" But when I looked around, the playground was empty.

Ten minutes had passed without my knowing it. Everyone had already gone back to their classrooms. And when I looked back up at the clouds, Jesus was gone.

I also went to revival meetings when I was growing up, and I saw amazing things. Our pastor, Brother Allen, laid his hands on people and healed them of all kinds of things. Growths on their arms would vanish.

They'd set their crutches aside and walk good as new again. Addictions disappeared.

My own father suffered from terrible migraine headaches. One time it was so bad he almost passed out. My mother finally took him to Brother Allen's revival meeting, and Brother Allen laid his hands on my dad's head. My dad blacked out. When he woke up again, he was healed. He never had another migraine again.

Meanwhile, life went on. My younger brother Jim and I made our way through Seaside Elementary School in Torrance, California, then South High School. We both worked part-time delivering the *Daily Breeze* newspaper and helping the bakers over at Angelo Revels Bakery. Every Sunday, our mother drove the two of us to church (our two younger sisters weren't born until later, and my older sister lived with my grandparents), and I was always glad to go. I just enjoyed the feeling of being at church.

I kept up my personal practice of faith, too. I had a Bible of my own that I kept next to my bed, and I read it for about half an hour every day. Each night before I went to sleep, I said a prayer to God. "Jesus

Christ, I thank you for my salvation. Please keep me and my family safe through the night. Amen."

I couldn't know, then, that those simple devotions were preparing me for the greatest test of my life.

* * *

I remember the day I got my draft notice. I was nineteen years old.

I pulled it out of the mailbox myself: a brown manila envelope from the United States government. I had a pretty good idea what it was before I opened it. *Oh, no* . . . I thought. *I hope this isn't what I think it is.*

But when I opened it, it said exactly what I knew it would say. "You have been drafted into the United States Army."

Before then, I hadn't thought much about the Vietnam War. I knew it was happening, but it seemed far away from me.

That draft notice changed everything.

There's no way to get out of this, I thought. So I decided not to try to fight it. Uncle Sam always said "I want *you*," and this time I knew he meant it.

I made my arrangements. My parents weren't happy that I was going off to war, but they knew I had no choice, and they supported me. I resigned from my first real job as a tank processor for Douglas Aircraft, where I had been working for about two years. "I'm sorry," I told my supervisor, "I'm not going to be here much longer than February 4."

I had a new job now.

* * *

The months I spent training between February and June 1969 were grueling.

I was assigned first to California's Fort Ord for basic training, then to Fort Sill in Oklahoma for advanced individual training in artillery. At Fort Ord, we trained from dawn to dusk: rise at four o'clock in the morning and run a couple of miles, breakfast at six o'clock, M14 target practice at the rifle range at seven o'clock, and on and on. We drilled in bivouacs and went on different kinds of combat training operations. I was elated to graduate from that place at the end of March, with my parents in attendance.

After a month of leave, I spent May and June at Fort Sill with forty other men, learning to fire 105-millimeter howitzer cannons. Those cannons were like miniature tanks. The first time I fired one, it almost knocked me down. The explosion was horrific. But I made it through that, too.

During those months of training, I kept my Bible with me. I read it whenever I found time—usually at night before bed, while the other guys were playing cards, telling stories, and talking about their girlfriends.

I was given another month of leave after Fort Sill. Then it was time to say goodbye.

My final farewell to California was a sailboat trip along the coast in Redondo Beach. I went with a girl I was dating at the time, Shannon—the sister of one of the guys I met at Fort Ord. The day was sunny and the sky was blue; coastal birds glided above us. We sailed along the shoreline, and I watched the houses and beaches go by, trying to burn them into my memory—just in case it was the last image I ever saw of my homeland.

Then I went home. I packed my Bible—a new Thompson Chain Reference Bible with a black binding that I'd bought from the Bible store the year before. I said goodbye to my parents for the last time. "This might be the last time you see me," I told them.

"I don't know what's going to happen over there in Vietnam."

"We'll write," they promised, "and we'll pray for you."

I got on a bus and headed up to the army base in Oakland. There, they gave me my duffel bag, my M16 rifle, my boots, my fatigues—all my gear. Then they put us on another bus to Travis Air Force Base.

I kissed the runway before I boarded the jumbo jet they had waiting for us.

Then I got on the plane.

As the jet taxied down the runway and lifted into the air, my stomach was full of butterflies. *This is it,* I thought. *There's no turning back.* People were dying in Vietnam, and I knew that I might be one of them. I was uncertain and a little bit afraid.

But I had confidence in God. And I was about to witness the power of that faith firsthand.

1/44TH ARTILLERY BRAVO BATTERY

Soldier standing next to a weapon carrier
on the base perimeter.

June 1970

Chapter 2

The First Miracle

*I can do all things through
Christ who strengthens me.*

−Philippians 4:13

I landed with 150 other soldiers at Benoit Air Force Base, Vietnam, on July 30, 1969.

We arrived around eight o'clock at night, and I could feel my heart hammering in my chest as the jumbo jet touched down. I was petrified. I didn't know what to expect. In my mind, I imagined myself stepping off the plane to a welcoming committee of gunfire, with bullets flying every which way.

In reality, there were no guns. Instead, there was darkness—and rain. This was the middle of the monsoon season. I walked off the jet into a thick wall of water and humidity. The air was hot and heavy with the dank smell of the tropics. Big signs were posted all over the base:

BEWARE OF ROCKET ATTACKS.
IN CASE OF SIRENS, TAKE COVER.

In seconds, the other soldiers and I were soaking wet. We ran for the hangar. There, they loaded us onto a green bus and took us to a holding station, where they assigned us to our new units in Vietnam.

My group was given orders to go to Cuea Viet near Quang Tri Province, close to the 17th parallel—about 150 miles north of the Benoit base.

We flew up there two days later. Everyone went to Dong Ha Combat Base, except for me and three other men trained to M.O.S. 13 Foxtrot 20. We piled into a Jeep and were taken to Charley Battery instead.

They needed us to fire the five 105 mm howitzer canons there.

Charley Battery was an old marine base that the army had taken over. At Charley Battery, the artillery guns fired from eight o'clock at night to five in the morning. The goal was to protect the infantry by targeting the area just in front of them.

The explosions kept the Vietnamese too far away to strike.

I didn't fire the guns right away. That first night on duty, I trained with the gunners. I was the ammo man. I stockpiled and loaded the live rounds: solid steel projectiles almost two feet long that weighed close to seventy pounds each. We only had a little bit of blue light to work by. Hours went by in the dark, stockpiling and loading round after round. It wasn't raining, but I was dripping wet with perspiration. Every time a howitzer went off, it rattled every bone in my body.

By the time my shift ended, I was exhausted. I made my way back to my new bed in the barracks. I made sure my Bible was on the little table next to it. I got down on my knees and said a prayer.

"God, please don't let my blood shed on this godforsaken soil," I prayed. "Save me from this war." Then I climbed into bed and fell asleep without another thought.

I didn't know that I was about to experience a miracle.

* * *

Two weeks passed.

We took turns firing the howitzers at night. When I wasn't on artillery duty, I was patrolling the perimeter or trying to sleep.

Sleeping wasn't easy. Now and then the explosions from the guns jarred me awake so badly that I fell out of my bed. Sometimes you couldn't tell the difference between the artillery firing at night and the sound of incoming mortars from the enemy. Often, we had to run for the bunkers in the dark to protect ourselves from enemy rocket fire.

It took me almost a month to get used to the idea that I was never going to get used to the gunfire. Every time the sun came up, I was happy just to be alive another day.

One mid-August morning, the sergeant found me in the barracks. "Private First Class Simmons," he said, "the captain wants you to drive the 548 cargo track out to the dump. You're to empty all the trash on the base. Take some soldiers with you." He gave me the names of the four other privates assigned to trash detail with me.

"Yes, sir," I said. The order was nothing unusual. I'd already driven the cargo track to the dump a few times. The dump itself was about six miles away, down a graded dirt road—just a big open landmass with nothing else around but a few bushes.

So I got my group together, and we started down the road: two of the other privates in the 548 with me, and two following behind us in a jeep with a short-wave radio and their M16 rifles—the usual escort.

We'd been driving for about three miles when we saw a group of four marines up ahead, walking in our direction. They had long poles with flat metal heads in their hands, and they were moving them across the dirt road. When they saw us coming, they stopped what they were doing. The four of them spread out in front of us to make a human road block.

Mine sweepers, I thought. *Shouldn't they be done for the day?* Almost every night and sometimes during the day, the Viet Cong planted mines on the roads. The mine sweepers cleared the mines twice every day: once in the morning, and again in the evening. As far as I knew, the morning check was done.

The four marines just stood there, waiting, until we drove up to meet them. As soon as I stopped the cargo track, the leader strode up to my window. Every line of his face was furious as he looked at me.

"Where in the heck do you think you're going, private?" he demanded.

I told him we were headed to the dump.

"Don't you know that this road hasn't been cleared for mines yet?" he shouted. "It's a miracle you weren't blown up! Who told you to come out here?"

"My . . . our captain gave orders to our sergeant for us to come out here and dump this trash," I told him, rattled. "I'm sorry. I didn't know that the road wasn't clear yet."

"Who is your captain?" the marine asked grimly. I told him. "I'm going to chew him out," he growled. "All of you could've been killed just now. Get back to base. We'll tell you when you have clearance to drive."

I turned the cargo track around, and we headed back down the road the way we'd come. None of us said anything. I knew the marine was right: it truly was a miracle we hadn't been blown up. Either there were no mines in the road that day, or they hadn't detonated.

Thank you, Jesus, for sparing our lives, I thought. *Thank you.*

That experience was harrowing for me. But it was only the beginning.

_____

108TH GROUP

PFC Paul W. Simmons driving a jeep.

December 1969

Chapter 3

THE SECOND MIRACLE

*Yea though I walk through the valley of
the shadow of death, I will fear no evil;
for You are with me; Your rod and
Your staff, they comfort me.*

—PSALM 23:4

After my near miss with the mines, four months passed in relative quiet. Which, in Vietnam, was not quiet at all.

Living in a war zone felt like being hunted. We were constantly on guard, ready to respond to sudden danger. And that put us in a state of stress, 24/7. You never knew what was going to happen from one moment to the next.

We didn't live from day to day in Vietnam. We lived from second to second.

In the second half of October, my unit was sent to patrol the A Shau Valley in Thua Thien Province for two weeks. We caravanned the 150 miles to the Laos border on Highway 1, with all five of our enormous self-propelled artillery guns in tow. Progress was slow going, and it took us three days to get there.

Agent Orange dusted the jungle that we traveled through and the ground we walked on. We filled up our water tank on wheels—the Water Buffalo—and drank from the rivers anyway, not knowing that the herbicide might affect our physical and mental health years later.

Halfway to A Shau, we passed a five-ton truck abandoned in the jungle down the side of a hill near the road. It was an army truck, OD green, with a white star on the side. Bamboo grass huts were scattered around it. There wasn't a soul in sight.

We passed it without a word. We knew a booby trap when we saw one.

No Viet Cong engaged us during the time we spent up there in A Shau Valley. By the time we arrived, they had gone back up to North Vietnam. I stood there in the valley where the famous Battle of Hamburger Hill had killed fifty marines and wounded hundreds more just months before, angry that a massacre like that had happened to anyone. All I could do was say a prayer for the men who had died.

* * *

After we returned to Cua Viet from the A Shau Valley, my path changed directions.

The army had orders to send my unit back to the United States. By then it was late 1969, and the government was starting to pull the military out of Vietnam. But my tour of duty wasn't over yet. I couldn't go home with the rest of Charley Battery.

Instead, I was transferred to the 108th Group at Dong Ha Combat Base, seven miles south of Quang Tri Province.

The Dong Ha base didn't have artillery guns. So when I arrived, I was assigned to a detail squad with ten other first-class privates instead. We did maintenance and took care of odd jobs, like policing the grounds and picking up trash and cigarette butts. We also pulled NCO duty, where we brought food to the sergeants' tables for them at lunchtime.

In the first week of December, our captain announced that he was looking for a volunteer to drive his jeep.

I was always ready for something new. "I volunteer, sir," I offered.

Captain Johnson nodded at me. I always looked neat and clean, with my clothes pressed and my shoes shined. That must have impressed him. "Private First Class Simmons, report to the office and pick up the keys for the jeep," he said. "You are now the new jeep driver."

"Thank you, sir," I saluted. And from then on, I was the base's official jeep driver.

I enjoyed driving the jeep. It wasn't just for the captain; I drove the NCOs and other officers around the base in it as well. The other guys taught me how to take care of it. Private Altoff from Arkansas showed me how to operate its shortwave radio. Private Rudy from Chicago showed me how to wipe it down with a rag and diesel fuel to get the OD-green paint to look brand new again. I bought him a cold Pepsi by way of thanks.

Then one morning in the second week of December, Captain Johnson asked me to drive him out to Con Thien Fire Base ten miles north of us.

"Yes, sir," I said. I didn't think anything of it. I knew he met with the other officers up there sometimes to take care of classified business.

I had no idea, when we set off down the road around ten o'clock, that we were driving straight into the path of another miracle.

It was just the two of us that day. Captain Johnson rode shotgun beside me, radioing in our Charlie Papas—checkpoints—as we sped along. The road was graded, with open space on either side. One hundred feet away to our right and left, tall, dense trees rose in the distance. The day was hot and humid, as usual. But it was also peaceful.

Then, as we approached our Romeo Bravo checkpoint, sniper fire opened on the Jeep.

We didn't have time to react. We didn't even have time to think. Pounding AK-47 gunfire shattered the quiet morning and suddenly bullets were flying all around us. They whined past my ears and over my head; they kicked up in the dirt on the right side of the jeep, trying to puncture the tires.

"Simmons, it's a sniper!" Captain Johnson shouted at me over the din. "What should we do?"

I kept my eyes fixed on the road. "I am going to keep driving this jeep, sir!" I shouted back.

Captain Johnson got back on the shortwave. "Charlie Papa, Red Barn, Romeo Bravo," he yelled over the gunfire. "We are under fire. I repeat, we are under fire . . ."

God, help us, I prayed, my hands gripping the steering wheel. *We're under attack.*

I didn't drive any faster. I didn't want to lose control of the jeep. In the middle of all that chaos, I just kept the vehicle moving right along as if nothing was happening.

And then, all at once, nothing was. The gunfire stopped. The bullets were gone. Everything looked just like it had a minute ago—a quiet, peaceful morning.

We had driven out of range of the sniper.

Captain Johnson got on the radio again. "Charlie Papa, we're clear. We made it," he said. That was all. He sat back in his seat, and the two of us didn't speak a word the rest of the way to Con Thien.

When we got there, Captain Johnson went off to his meeting. I waited for him quietly in the jeep, alone, reflecting. We'd just driven through a cloud of gunfire like sitting ducks, yet we had both walked away without a scratch. Even the jeep was unscathed—not a single bullet hole in it, let alone its tires. It was as if God Himself had intervened and directed the bullets away from us.

Thank you, God, for hearing my prayers, I prayed, over and over again. I didn't care how many times I said it, just as long as He heard. *Thank you for bringing us through that horror alive. Thank you, thank you, thank you . . .*

108th Group

Private First Class Paul W. Simmons
standing by the barracks.

December 1969

Chapter 4

THE THIRD MIRACLE

Perfect love casts out fear.

–1 JOHN 4:18

That December in Vietnam was the first Christmas I'd spent away from my family.

I was homesick every day in that country. Now and then we were allowed to call our relatives back in the States for up to an hour, and we wrote letters back and forth. One day I went to the Post Exchange—the PX—and bought two cassette players with matching tapes. I recorded a message on one of the tapes and sent it to my family, along with some extra blank tapes and the second cassette player. They listened to my tape when it got there. Then they recorded a message themselves and sent a tape back. We did that back and forth, and it was good to hear their voices.

But even though those messages from California helped, my homesickness was even worse during the holiday. I thought about the celebration that would be happening back home: setting up the tree and decorations, eating our baked ham dinner and trimmings, attending church on Christmas Eve and Christmas Sunday. I wished I was there with the people I loved, instead of in Vietnam.

Even so, we did the best we could with what we had. One day about a week before Christmas, Rudy—the same guy who showed me how to wipe down the jeep with diesel fuel to make the paint shine—had an idea. "Hey Paul," he said to me. "Let's dig up a Christmas tree. We can decorate it right here in the barracks."

"Okay," I agreed.

So the two of us headed out behind the unit and found a small tree, maybe five feet tall. It wasn't a pine—it had lots of thin branches and tiny green leaves—but we figured it would do. Rudy and I dug it up and carried it back to the barracks. There, we decorated it with used ammo caps, the string from old wrappings, and paper that we colored red and green. We gathered the care packages from everyone's families and put them under the tree—presents for the 108th Group.

It wasn't home, but it lifted our spirits. And the good Lord always let me know that he was on our side. That Christmas, like every other day in Vietnam, my Bible was the greatest gift of all.

* * *

About a month had passed since the sniper had opened fire on Captain Johnson and me in the jeep. Like everyone else, I'd been keeping busy.

We always had something to do.

We patrolled and kept the place clean. At one point, about ten of us spent a month building a motor pool garage. Most of the time we worked four days a week and had the other three days off. Even when we were off, we helped around the base.

But I did have some free time to myself. Some of it I used for my devotions. Some of it I spent doing odds and ends.

Once, a guy in my unit gave me a broken ice box that he didn't want anymore. I fixed its wire cord with some electrical tape, and from then on I had a working ice box. I sold cold Pepsis to the other soldiers for fifty cents each.

I also got to know the local Vietnamese culture a little bit. A few women had market huts with grass hats set up on the base—just four or five them. They sold us souvenirs: trinkets, beads, handmade fans, rice candy, dish sets to send back to our families in the States.

Usually the Vietnamese ladies struck up conversations with us while we were shopping. "What kind of food do you eat back in the United States?" a girl vendor asked me once.

"My favorite is a hamburger, fries, and a Coke to drink from McDonald's hamburger restaurant," I told her. I wondered if I'd ever taste that meal again.

Once in a while, six or seven of us drove over to a massage parlor in the nearest Vietnamese village to get massages from the young girl-sans there. The girl-sans were very light and small; they walked along our backs and rubbed our necks and shoulders. It felt wonderful, since we were always tired and tense.

However, we weren't careless about visiting those massage parlors. One of us would drive a long-barrel gun on tracks up to the place and aim it at the door, ready to blow the building up if the others didn't come back out alive. But thankfully, we never had to fire that gun, and the massages continued to be great stress relief.

* * *

The third miracle arrived on a warm Thursday in the middle of January.

That morning, one of our sergeants strode into the barracks. "We need eight of you to go to Phu Bai for detail work," he said. "This is just for the day—routine maintenance. Cleaning up the buildings, basic repairs. Private First Class Simmons, you're up." He appointed seven other guys to go along with me. Then, "Get going," he ordered.

We got going. Phu Bai wasn't far from us—only about seven miles away. We arrived by ten o'clock and started on the maintenance. They needed some work done on their barracks.

We were hanging a door, passing screwdrivers and hammers back and forth between us, when they called us for lunch at half past eleven.

Oh good, I thought, *lunch.* I always had a healthy appetite, and my stomach was starting to growl.

We filed into the mess hall and lined up at the serving counter. It was a quiet day; nobody had much of anything to say, except to tell the server what kind of food they wanted on their plates. I waited with an empty tray in my hands until it was my turn, smelling the fresh roast beef, broccoli, and corn.

"What'll you have?" he asked me when the line moved up.

"I'll take some corn . . . " I started.

He had just shoveled a big spoonful of it onto my plate when the uproar started.

"Incoming!" someone shouted. "Incoming!"

We knew what that meant: a hailstorm of rockets and mortars was headed straight for us.

The shout spread like wildfire. In seconds, everyone was yelling "Incoming!"—me included. All of us dropped our food, adding an avalanche of crashing plates to the chaos. We ran for the door, slipping and sliding over the mess of corn, chocolate cake, soda pop, and orange juice. I almost fell, but pushed myself up again before my body had time to land, and kept moving. There wasn't time to waste on hitting the floor.

Outside, I realized I didn't have time to make it to the bunkers twenty yards away. Around me, soldiers were taking cover behind anything they could find. I did the same thing and dove for the first thing I saw: a big pile of 4×4 wood beams.

Another soldier standing nearby had the same idea and landed behind the pile next to me. We crouched low on the ground together with our hands over our heads.

"I'm Private First Class Paul W. Simmons," I shouted over the chaos, "from Torrance, California."

"Private John Ryan," he shouted back. "Wichita Falls, Texas."

"John," I told him, "if we live through this, look me up in Torrance."

"I will," he agreed. "You look me up also."

That was all we had time to say before the mortars came down.

A saying I know goes, "There are no atheists in a foxhole." For me and John Ryan, that was the honest truth. We both started praying together as the rockets came down around us, one after another—about twenty of them, all told. The sound was huge and horrific, a nightmare. It filled my ears and shook every bone in my body. I felt like jet engines were coming down on top of us; like we were trapped at the heart of the biggest thunderstorm on earth. We could hear the trees around the base cracking and crashing down through the explosions.

That attack seemed to last forever. In reality, it was over in just a few minutes.

We didn't move right away, after the explosions stopped. We stayed on the ground behind those wooden beams for five or ten minutes to make sure the Viet Cong weren't going to fire any more rockets or mortars. Only then, we slowly stood up and looked around. When we did, I couldn't believe what I saw.

Nothing was damaged. The mess hall was still intact.

Everything looked just as it had before.

Around me, the other soldiers were also gradually coming out of their makeshift barricades. Nobody said anything, and not a single person was hurt. They all looked as shocked as I was.

Slowly, we all went back to what we'd been doing before. I helped clean up the food on the floor in the mess hall, but I didn't eat lunch that day. I was sick to my stomach. Most of us had lost our appetites.

I went back to work on the barracks knowing that, once again, God had heard our prayers and saved our lives.

1/44TH ARTILLERY BRAVO BATTERY

Corporal Paul W. Simmons drinking a Pepsi
at the table next to the mess hall.

March 1970

Chapter 5

THE FOURTH MIRACLE

*Faith cometh by hearing
and hearing by the word of God.*

–ROMANS 10:17

In December 1969, I started to notice problems with my hearing.

My ears were always ringing. I could hear the sound of the artillery guns from my first assignment at Charley Battery going off, even though I didn't work them anymore. It was a constant *Boom! Boom! Boom!* When people talked to me, I had to ask them to repeat themselves.

By the time they transferred me to the 1st and 44th Artillery—Bravo Battery at Dong Ha Combat Base—in February 1970, the problem was bad enough that I knew I had to do something about it.

As soon as I arrived at Bravo Base, I went to see my new master sergeant—Joseph Clayton Sanders, an impeccably groomed man who had a good heart under his very strict exterior. I didn't even wait to be assigned to my new bed in the barracks first. I left my things in a holding area and went straight to him. "Sir," I told him, "I can't hear well out of my ears, sir."

Master Sergeant Sanders didn't waste time. The next thing I knew, I was on my way to the Repose Hospital Ship off of the Gulf of Tonkin.

A Huey chopper picked me up at the Quang Tri airstrip a few miles away from the base, and we took off for the Repose. I watched rice paddies and villages fly by four thousand feet below us. A door gunner manned a loaded .50-caliber machine gun that hung over the left side of the chopper.

Finally, after about twenty minutes, we touched down on the front of the ship. I stepped out onto the tarmac, and the chopper took off again. One of the naval personnel on deck escorted me into the ship, down a corridor to the doctor's small, steel-chamber office. Then the doctor himself had me sit on the examination table while I explained what I was there for. He looked at my ears.

"Private Simmons," he told me after a minute, "I find that you have some hearing loss in both ears. I'm going to give you a doctor's note about this to give to your master sergeant in command."

Under other circumstances, it would've troubled me to learn that I had hearing loss at just nineteen years old. But Vietnam was a war zone. I was just happy to be alive, and I was grateful to the doctor for seeing me. I looked around the office for a way to thank him.

"Sir," I asked, "could I take out the trash for you?"

The doctor looked up from the note he was writing. "Sure," he said. "Thank you. The receptacle is down the hall and to the left."

I dumped the trash and came back. He handed me my note, and I shook his hand and thanked him. Then I went to the galley for lunch and flipped through a magazine from home until the Huey chopper returned to take me back to shore.

I made it back to Bravo Battery that same afternoon, and Master Sergeant Sanders was giving out assignments.

"Private First Class Simmons," he said, approaching me by my newly assigned bed in the barracks, "I'm assigning you to the Quad 50s."

The Quad 50s were also called "Dusters." They were four .50-caliber machine guns mounted on top of a five-ton open-bed truck. This was a field assignment, and I knew that I'd be a liability out there. If someone snuck up behind us, I wouldn't hear them. I couldn't warn or protect the other guys.

"Sir, I think I'll be a risk out there," I admitted.

"Why?" Master Sergeant Sanders demanded. "What's wrong with you?"

I handed him the doctor's note. He took it and read it in silence. Then, "Private Simmons," he said, "You are relieved of your duties out in the field.

"I am reassigning you to mess hall duty as a cook."

* * *

As far as Vietnam went, cooking in the mess hall was the best job I could have gotten.

I learned to cook in my mother's kitchen, and I always liked cooking. My favorite recipe was her meatloaf dinner. When Master Sergeant Sanders assigned me to the mess hall, I went into the pantry and took stock of what I had to work with. I found boxes full of recipes—good ones—already typed up and ready to go. *Wow,* I thought, *these are great.*

I took those recipes and improvised to make them better. I also taught the other guys in the kitchen— Hobo and Wayne Parks—how to make my mother's meatloaf. The three of us were on duty every other day. We cooked three hundred plates of food—breakfast, lunch, and dinner—from four in the morning to four in the afternoon.

Before long, our meatloaf was famous. Officers came by and asked our mess sergeant if we were the ones cooking that day. One night, the other guys in our unit broke into the mess hall and raided the freezer for frozen meatloaves. But the meatloaves were rock-solid, and they couldn't warm them up—so they started throwing them around like footballs instead. Watching them, I had to laugh.

I enjoyed cooking, but I worked hard in the mess hall. One afternoon in early March, I was alone in the kitchen, just getting ready to call it a day, when Mess Sergeant Easton walked in. He didn't say anything at first—just stopped and took a look around. Then, "Private First Class Simmons?" he said.

"Yes, sir?" I replied.

"I don't think this floor looks clean enough," he told me. "You can't leave yet. I want you to get a bucket and start scrubbing this floor until it's clean enough to eat on."

I was tired after twelve straight hours of cooking hundreds of meals in the high-humidity heat. I had started at four o'clock that morning. The other guys and I were responsible for cleaning the kitchen, but papa-sans and mama-sans usually scrubbed the mess-hall floors. However, none of that mattered. My sergeant had just given me an order.

I got a bucket of soap water and a scrub brush, and I started scrubbing the floor.

Sergeant Easton stood there and watched me as I worked. I put my back into it, but it didn't seem to make a difference. After an hour, he was still standing there, and I was still scrubbing.

"Sergeant Easton . . . " I ventured, "the papa-sans and mama-sans usually take care of this. I'm pretty tired, sir."

"I don't care about that," Sergeant Easton said. "I want you to do it." So I just kept scrubbing.

Another brutal hour of that went by. I was sweating, sore, and exhausted. Finally, right when I thought I was going to be scrubbing the mess hall floor all night, Sergeant Easton smiled. "Okay, Private First Class Simmons, that's enough. You can stop."

"Yes, sir." I dropped the scrub brush in the bucket and slowly pushed myself up off the floor. I had no idea why he'd been disciplining me—until he spoke again.

"Private Simmons, because you obeyed my orders, I'm going to put in for you to receive another stripe. You're moving up in rank to Corporal Simmons."

And I left the mess hall that day smiling after all.

* * *

It had been eight weeks since the bombing at Phu Bai. The miracle I experienced there had shocked me. But it didn't come close to what happened during the second week of March 1970.

At eight o'clock in the evening, I received a call from Master Sergeant Sanders. "Corporal Simmons," he said, "come to my office on the base. I have orders for you."

So I headed over to his office. It was a warm, quiet, dark night—not too many people around. When I got to his door, I knocked, and he told me to come in.

"Corporal Simmons," he greeted me.

"Sir," I replied, walking into the well-lit room. "You have orders for me?" Then I stood in front of his desk as Master Sergeant Sanders relayed instructions to me for the next day: what to do in the mess hall, what to clean up, what food to prepare—the usual.

I was listening to him carefully, taking mental notes on his instructions, when something unexplainable happened.

My body froze stock-still.

I couldn't move anything but my eyes. And that wasn't all. I suddenly realized that I couldn't hear anything, either. Master Sergeant Sanders was still in front of me giving his orders, and I could see his mouth going—but there was no sound.

Then, before I could think how to react, my master sergeant stopped talking and leapt out of his chair. He started waving his arms, and I could tell by the way his mouth moved that he was shouting at me, but I couldn't hear a word. My lips couldn't move to say anything in reply, either. A split second later, Master Sergeant Sanders ran for the door of the office and disappeared from my line of vision.

The lights went out.

Paralyzed and terrified in the pitch-blackness of that empty office, a single sound broke the silence: the telltale whistle of a rocket. I listened to it grow louder and louder.

That's what he was trying to say, I realized. He was telling me to get to the bunker.

Then the whistling stopped.

I was trained to know that when you hear the whistling of a rocket stop, it means the rocket is coming in right on top of you—and it's going to be a direct hit. But I was still powerless to move.

When the rocket connected with the office, it seemed to happen in slow motion. The bright white light of the explosion bloomed horribly the dark. It started on the floor just feet in front of me and grew into a cigar shape, rising into the air. I watched it get bigger and bigger, higher and higher.

Then, suddenly, everything sped up.

The blinding light of the explosion swallowed me. I saw pieces of white-hot shrapnel flying right at my face.

Then I lost consciousness, and everything went dark.

Days went by in that darkness, but I didn't learn that until later. While it was happening, I had no sense of time. I had no sense of anything.

When I finally woke up again, I was working in the mess hall.

I had no recollection of how I'd gotten there. One minute I was in the darkness following that explosion, and the next I was standing in the kitchen with a broom in my hands, sweeping the floor. There wasn't so much as a scratch on my body, and it was around lunchtime. Hobo and Wayne Parks were going about their business. No one paid any special attention to me.

I paused for a moment with that broom in my hands. Then I just kept on sweeping the floor.

I couldn't process what had happened to me. There was no acceptable explanation. The deep shock that settled in was really a defense mechanism. I didn't ask anyone what had happened. I didn't ask where I'd been for the four or five days that I was unconscious. I didn't even talk to God about it. I couldn't. All I could do was keep my hands busy. If I had tried to think about what had happened to me right then, I would have lost my mind.

I will never fully understand that fourth miracle in Vietnam. To this day, only one thing is clear to me: something divine in nature got me through it.

1/40TH ARTILLERY CHARLIE BATTERY

Soldier standing by barracks at Cua Viet.

August 1969

Chapter 6

THE FIFTH MIRACLE

*Be not forgetful to entertain strangers:
for thereby some have
entertained angels unawares.*

−HEBREWS 13:2

I say that I experienced seven miracles in Vietnam. But the truth is, between the lines of those seven big events, smaller miracles were always happening.

Around the third week of March 1970, Wayne Parks and I were making breakfast in the mess hall. We got the hash browns, eggs, and sausage cooking on the stove, and Wayne started brewing coffee. I took stock of what was missing. Then, "I'll go get the orange juice," I said.

We kept all the fruit juices outside in an icebox by the side of the building. I headed out there. It was about four o'clock in the morning—still dark out, but the ice box and the door to the mess hall were lit by flood lights. No one was around. The rest of the unit was still sound asleep.

I dug the orange juice out and closed the icebox up again. Then I turned to go back inside.

Someone was standing by the mess hall door.

He was a well-groomed young man in green fatigues, with neatly combed black hair and a kind smile on his face. I hadn't heard anyone walk up, and I'd never seen him before. On the surface he looked normal enough, but there was something different about him that I couldn't put my finger on.

"Good morning. Can I get you something to eat or drink?" I asked him.

"No thanks," he replied.

"Would you like to come in and sit down for a while?"

"No," he said, still smiling as he looked at me. "But thank you."

So I gave him a nod and went on my way with the orange juice. Just before I went inside, I looked back over my shoulder at the place where he'd been standing.

He was gone.

I looked for him the next day. But he was nowhere to be found—not in my unit, and not in the surrounding units. He vanished just as quickly as he appeared.

Then, months later—after I returned home from Vietnam—I went to visit my grandmother, and I saw a picture on her bedroom wall that I'd never noticed before. "Who's this?" I asked her.

"That's my son," she told me, "Little Ed."

Little Ed became a Christian at a very young age, and he used to witness to a friend of his, Tommy Smith. One day, when the two of them were about twelve years old, Little Ed was over at Tommy's house while Mr. and Mrs. Smith were away. Tommy found a .22 rifle. He didn't know it was loaded. As a joke, he aimed it at Little Ed and pulled the trigger.

Little Ed died instantly, shot through the heart. My grandparents never pressed charges, since it was clear that Little Ed's death was an accident.

As I looked at his picture on the wall, I realized why he seemed so familiar.

He looked exactly like the man I'd seen outside the mess hall, that morning in Vietnam.

Little Ed's angel had visited me there, at four o'clock in the morning, to bring me God's blessing—and Godspeed.

* * *

Meeting Little Ed wasn't the only "small miracle" that happened in Vietnam.

Toward the end of March, Master Sergeant Sanders approached me out on the grounds of Dong Ha Combat Base. "Corporal Simmons," he told me, "you've been serving in Vietnam for eight months. You're entitled to two weeks of R&R outside the country—anywhere you want. Where are you going to go?"

I thought about it for a moment. Then I replied, "Sir, I cannot go on a two-week R&R out of the country."

He lifted his eyebrows. "Why not, Corporal Simmons?" he demanded.

"Because if I leave Vietnam, sir," I answered honestly, "I will go AWOL. I won't come back at all. I don't trust myself."

Master Sergeant Sanders nodded. "You can take a week off in country instead, then," he said. "Go to Da Nang."

I went to Da Nang.

The week I spent there did me a lot of good. We never had a moment completely to ourselves on base. In Da Nang, I sat and watched the Huey helicopters taking off and landing on the nearby runway. I lay in a cot and read my Bible. I felt a little peace.

When I came back in the first week of April, I learned that things had been anything but quiet while I was away.

"Simmons," said Mess Sergeant Meyers when he saw me. "We're glad to see you back." In the few days that I'd been gone, a series of rocket attacks had bombarded Bravo Battery. They all knew that I had a lot of faith in God and that He'd saved me from my share of close calls in the past.

"We thought we were going to die," Meyers told me as we walked to my barracks together. "Me and the other guys were praying. We told God that if he brought you back alive, we'd stop smoking, cursing, and drinking beer."

When we got to my bed, I saw plywood hammered over the middle of my headboard.

"Look at this," Sergeant Meyers said. He bent to pick something up. Next thing I knew, I was holding a five-pound piece of thick, twisted iron shrapnel. It was about the size of two dinner plates, and each end was curled into sharp claws.

"That went through your headboard while you were gone," commented Sergeant Meyers.

I just stared from the shrapnel to the headboard and back again. If I had been sleeping in the bed that night, the white-hot metal would have cut my head right off. God had spared my life once again.

After my return, the rockets stopped falling on Bravo Battery.

* * *

Six weeks had passed since my experience with the explosion and the time warp. I didn't think life could get any stranger than that—even in a warzone. But when the fifth miracle happened on a Tuesday in the fourth week of April 1970, it was the most mentally devastating one of them all.

That morning started out like any other. As usual, I was on my way to Master Sergeant Sanders to report for duty. No one else was around.

I was walking across the open space toward the master sergeant's office when, suddenly, a Huey Cobra fighter helicopter lifted off the ground a few hundred feet away—and flew straight at me.

Everything happened in a split second. But I remember every detail as if it had taken place in slow motion.

The pilot in the Cobra was close enough to see clearly. He was well groomed and wearing a U.S. Army uniform, obviously an officer—and the look on his face was as cold as stone. I had never seen him before, but I didn't have time to question who he was or what he was doing on our base. I didn't have time to react at all.

I vividly remember the moment he pushed the red button on the stick in his cockpit, and opened fire on me.

John Wayne can get away with dodging bullets in the movies. But in real life, you can't dodge the bullets. In that split second of time, I stood frozen where I was, hypnotized with shock. I couldn't believe what was happening, even though my mind was extremely alert and clear. My eyes were glued to the barrage of "friendly" fire kicking up dirt on a beeline toward me. I watched it come straight up to my feet, my chest, and I knew that I was going to die. I felt my internal organs shutting down.

Then, as I stared down at the barrage, I saw the impossible. The line of huge helicopter bullets speeding directly toward the insides of my ankles and lower legs broke apart into tiny pieces, and changed directions. I watched as they curved around my left boot and then shot out perpendicularly to the side instead of hitting me.

The higher bullets that should have buried themselves in my chest never hit, either, and those ones didn't go around my body, even in pieces. They disintegrated altogether.

It was like something out of an episode of *Star Trek*. As if God's angel had put a force field around my body.

Meanwhile, the helicopter never stopped. The trail of friendly fire continued over my head and hit the outhouse behind me, making a piercing noise as the bullets hit the tin roof. I managed to turn my head. When I did, I saw the Cobra flying away—and Private Wilkinson stumbling out of the outhouse with his pants hanging down.

"Corporal Simmons!" he called out, trying to get his pants up. "Are you all right?"

I couldn't speak. The extreme shock of what I'd just been through had paralyzed me. Hundreds of bullet marks left a trail leading up to the place I stood, and after it. But I was fine. There wasn't so much as a hole in my fatigues.

I was supposed to die that day. God made a way where there wasn't a way.

DA NANG NEW UNIT
1/44TH ARTILLERY BRAVO BATTERY

Cooks peeling potatoes for dinner
in front of the new mess hall.

September 1970

Chapter 7

THE SIXTH MIRACLE

For God so loved the world that He gave His only
begotten Son, that whoever believeth in
Him should not perish but have everlasting life.

–JOHN 3:16

The wildlife in Vietnam was like something out of a horror movie.

We used the bunkers often to protect ourselves from incoming rockets. One day, as I ran down into them to escape an attack of falling mortars, a rat as big as a Chihuahua came sprinting straight at me. I jumped into the air and it flew under my feet, its long tail swinging back and forth as it went.

Another time, coming out of a shower, I reached for my towel and two mating cockroaches the size of baseballs sank their teeth into my finger. I yelled and yanked my hand back as they flew out of hiding and buzzed around the room; my finger turned red and throbbed for hours afterward. All of our beds in the barracks came with mosquito nets to keep us from getting eaten alive in our sleep.

For all that, though, and despite the fact that we were living in a war zone, we did what we could to keep our spirits up in Vietnam.

Sometimes, when we weren't being hit by rockets, we watched movies. On Thursday nights, twenty or twenty-five of us would set up a white projector screen and watch John Wayne films together. We made a night of it, with Pepsi and popcorn to go along with the show. But we also kept grenades in our pockets and had our M16s ready, just in case.

Other times, I borrowed a mini television from one of the other guys and watched my favorite show: *Star Trek*. I admired William Shatner, and on some level I think I related to the stories. The *Star Trek* crew was hopping from world to world, surviving in strange places. I was surviving in a strange place, too.

Food was another thing. Once in a while our mess sergeants threw a barbecue for the soldiers. They made barbecue pits of fifty-gallon barrels sawed in half and filled the barrels with charcoal briquettes. Then we barbecued steaks and chicken, poured beer over the meat, and brushed the whole thing with barbecue sauce.

One time, the Army actually flew in ice cream for us from the States. That was a real treat, because we never had ice cream in Vietnam. We couldn't even get real milk. So when they flew in a big case of vanilla ice cream in a Chinook helicopter to boost morale, we were excited. We knew how expensive it was, flying that fresh ice cream out to us for fourteen hours on dry ice. We had an ice cream party.

Some of the other soldiers got mixed up with drugs, since they could buy them cheap from the ma-ma-sans. But I was never one of them. Instead, I took up a hobby: photography.

It happened by accident. One day I stumbled across a photography darkroom over in the far left-hand corner of the base. Nobody else seemed to be using it. So I thought, *Hey, this can be my hobby.*

I went to the PX and bought a special slow-shutter frame camera and some expensive film. Then I went around the base taking pictures. I photographed the surroundings, the other guys—anything I wanted.

After that, I took the negatives back to the darkroom and developed them. I gave pictures to anyone who wanted one, and they thought it was a pretty nice thing I was doing. I enjoyed it, too.

But no matter what we did, the stress of living in Vietnam never really went away.

* * *

The sixth miracle arrived in the second week of June 1970—a month and a half after the Cobra helicopter pilot opened fire on me.

It was about half past four on a Tuesday morning, and Wayne Parks and I were in the mess hall preparing breakfast. Wayne was rinsing some of the salt off of the canned bacon we planned to serve with pancakes and powdered eggs. I was frying potatoes on the stove. The base was dark and quiet. No one else was awake that early.

Suddenly, a sound pierced the silence.

It began as a high, undulating whistle. Then it grew louder and lower—until it sounded like a freight train coming down on top of us. I could practically hear the *ding, ding, ding* of a train-crossing sound in my ears.

A second later, that incoming rocket hit the roof of the mess hall above us.

It should have blown us to smithereens. That's what rockets are designed to do. They blow up buildings when they hit them.

Instead, this rocket bounced off the roof.

We heard the huge, dull *thud* it made as it connected. The mess hall shook. Windows rattled in their panes and spices hummed on the shelves. But even though the impact we felt was big, it should've been bigger for a rocket coming in at that speed—even one that didn't explode. The windows should've shattered, and everything on the kitchen shelves should've fallen right off. Instead, the impact was muffled—as though we were somehow insulated against the blow.

Meanwhile, the rocket kept going. It hit the roof with so much momentum that it flew another two hundred yards before landing in an empty field next to the base. I heard it blow up—a loud, reverberating *BOOM*.

That was huge, I thought. *It must have been a 122 mm rocket.*

Wayne and I stopped what we were doing and looked at each other mutely for a moment, shaken.

To this day I'm not sure he understood what had happened to us, but I did. I bowed my head and said a prayer. *Thank you, dear Lord, for placing your hand on the roof and keeping that rocket from blowing up on top of us. Thank you for saving our lives again.*

Then Wayne and I simply went on making breakfast. The base was still quiet. No one else had heard the 122 explode off in the field, and there were no other rockets. In an hour and a half, dozens of hungry soldiers would come filing in, as usual. They still needed to eat.

Just because I was almost blown up didn't mean I could stop cooking.

* * *

A few days later, Master Sergeant Sanders pushed open the door to the mess hall. "Come out here," he called to us cooks in the kitchen. "I want you to witness something."

It was about half past ten in the morning. *What's going on?* I wondered. But I just put down the bread I was holding and followed the other guys outside.

When we got out there and joined him, Master Sergeant Sanders simply said, "Look up."

We looked up.

American B-52 bombers were flying over our heads, four thousand feet up in the air. As we watched, they flew several miles over the border between North and South Vietnam—the 17th parallel—and dropped cigar-shaped Napalm bombs on the northern side. We were too far away to hear the explosions, but we saw the flames rise up into the sky as the bombs struck.

I had seen MiG fighter jets come in on the big hill by our base and fire rounds at the enemy before, rarely. But never anything like this. I felt conflicted as I stood there, watching. On one hand, I knew that that attack was giving us a measure of protection. On the other hand, it was truly horrific to behold. But at the end of the day, it didn't matter how I felt about it.

We were killing the Viet Cong.

Da Nang 1/44th Artillery Bravo Battery

Flags and supplies unloading at the new unit.

August 1970

Chapter 8

THE SEVENTH MIRACLE

For He has said,
I will never leave thee,
nor forsake thee.

–HEBREWS 13:5

Almost three weeks after the 122 rocket bounced off the roof of the Bravo Battery mess hall, in the first week of July 1970, I experienced my seventh and final miracle in Vietnam.

It began one morning when Master Sergeant Sanders found me in the mess hall and ordered, "Corporal Simmons, take the five-ton army truck and go pick up food rations at the depot in Quang Tri Province."

I had never gone to pick up rations before. Usually the mess sergeant assigned the task to a different licensed private than me, along with someone else to sit in the passenger seat with a shotgun, just in case. But I wasn't one to question my master sergeant's orders.

"Yes, sir," I said, and headed out to the motor pool. I didn't even think to ask for someone to ride shotgun. I found the five-ton truck, climbed into the driver's seat, and went on my way.

The road to Quang Tri was about seven miles long and wide enough for about one-and-a-half cars, with low brush and empty space stretching away into the distance on either side. It was graded dirt—completely flat. I kept my foot on the gas pedal the whole time, driving about thirty miles per hour.

Then, about five-and-a-half miles into the trip, just as I was approaching a small bridge, two Vietnamese soldiers riding Honda 50cc motorbikes came up behind me on the road.

They looked like ARVNs—South Vietnamese soldiers who were allies of the United States. But we never really knew whether the Vietnamese we interacted with were actually on our side or not. Some of them worked for the Viet Cong at the same time they were working for us. I watched the soldiers on the motorbikes cautiously as they drew up alongside my army truck and kept going. They seemed like they were just going to pass me up.

Instead, they zig-zagged in front of me, slowed down, and stopped in the middle of the road—all in the space of three seconds.

I slammed on the brakes for the first time since climbing into the truck back at Bravo Base, and that was when I heard it: the dull, horrible sound of metal grinding on metal.

The brakes were out.

My five-ton army truck ran right over the two Vietnamese soldiers and their motorbikes with a sickening *thud.*

Five more Vietnamese soldiers appeared nearby and opened fire, aiming their M16 rifles over the roof of the army truck's cab. They weren't aiming to kill—yet. But if those bullets had been words, they would have said "Beware: you're just about dead."

Meanwhile, I was still frantically trying to stop the truck. I pumped the brakes, but felt nothing but metal—the brake pads were completely shot-through. I yanked on the emergency brake. That didn't help much, either. It seemed like forever before the truck finally coasted to a stop and the rifle fire ceased.

I shoved open the door and leapt out to look under the truck. The two soldiers and their bikes were there, badly mangled. One of them wasn't moving at all. The other's head was going up and down in torment.

I stood up and looked around for help, my heart pounding in my ears. On the bridge twenty feet ahead of me, I saw two CBs—Navy Construction Battalion Engineers—out for routine maintenance. I ran over to them. One had a shortwave radio in his hand. "Call for help!" I shouted at him. "Call—call the hospital or an ambulance or something. There's been an accident. Two ARVN soldiers are down." Then I turned and sprinted back to the truck to see if I could do anything to help the run-down ARVNs.

The next thing I knew I was surrounded by the five ARVN soldiers, every one of them pointing an M16 rifle at my head. I could see in their faces that they were ready to pull the triggers.

I thought I was going to die.

Then a Vietnamese soldier dressed in a black uniform stepped forward—the leader of the group. I heard the men with the M16s ask him, in Vietnamese, if they should kill me. He shook his head. "Wait!" he ordered in English, and no one pulled a trigger. But they didn't lower their guns either.

The soldier in black looked at me. "What is your name?" he asked.

"Corporal Paul W. Simmons," I told him honestly. I felt horrible about what had just happened to those two soldiers. I was willing to do everything I could to cooperate.

The leader kept asking me questions, and at first I willingly answered them all. But then the questions got personal. "Where do you live? What are your relatives' names? Which unit are you with? How many soldiers are in your unit? What are the names of your officers?"

When he started asking me classified information about my unit, I knew that I wasn't just being questioned. I was being interrogated. And there was every chance that I was about to be taken prisoner of war.

I changed my mode. From that point on, I became a robot. Every question he asked me, I responded the same way: with my name, rank, and serial number.

We kept that up for the next forty-five minutes. The CBs on the bridge were powerless to interfere. I couldn't even see them from where I was standing.

Then, suddenly, two jeeps pulled up next to my interrogation group and stopped. Everyone in them was armed and aiming weapons at us.

It was the Army military police.

A wave of joy and relief went through me. *Thank God for the CBs on the bridge*, I thought; they had radioed for help. I watched as one of the MPs exited a jeep and strode up to us, keeping his .45 caliber pistol aimed at the group. "Back away from him," he told the Vietnamese soldiers, and they did. Then he looked at me. "What's your name and what unit are you with?" he demanded.

"My name is Corporal Paul Simmons, E-4," I replied. "I'm with Bravo Battery at the 1/44th Artillery Base. My master sergeant in command is Joseph Clayton Sanders."

The MP nodded and sent a radio dispatch asking for my unit. When he got through, he told them to connect him with Master Sergeant Sanders. I heard the master sergeant come on the line. "You need to get out here to the bridge and pick up Corporal Paul Simmons," the MP said into the radio. "He's had an accident near Quang Tri and he's in trouble."

I stood there with the MPs for several minutes until Master Sergeant Sanders arrived. When he did, I thanked them and joined my master sergeant in his jeep.

"What happened?" he asked me when I got inside.

I told him the whole story, and added, "I think I killed those two ARVN soldiers, sir." Thinking about them made me feel sick. I still didn't know whether those men were alive or dead—nor would I ever know.

Master Sergeant Sanders gave an odd, tight kind of smile. "That's what happened, huh?" he said.

"Yes, sir." I didn't know what else to tell him, since every word had been the truth.

We drove back to Bravo Battery in silence.

When I returned to the barracks, the other guys started kidding around with me about the fact that I'd killed two Vietnamese soldiers. But I didn't think it was funny. "This is serious," I said. "I didn't want to kill them. It was an accident." I was still shocked and hurting inside. I asked them to stop, and they laid off me after that.

I knew how lucky I was to be alive. When the others had wandered off, I got on my knees by my bed.

"Dear God," I said quietly, "I'm sorry I killed those two soldiers. Please forgive me for that. Thank you for saving my life, and for keeping me from becoming a prisoner of war of the Viet Cong. Thank you."

* * *

Three months later, on September 9, 1970, I left Vietnam for good.

In the time before I left, the entire Bravo Battery unit moved from Dong Ha Combat Base to Da Nang, near the 17th parallel—a 150-mile trip that took more than two weeks to make. We arrived in Da Nang the first week of August. Our mess sergeants Collins and Meyers and us five cooks kept busy all through that hot summer month, taking turns cooking in our new mess hall.

Then, finally, it was September.

The week before I left, I said my goodbyes. Everyone was a little different.

Mess Sergeant Steve Collins threw me a going away party. Really, it was a potato-peeling party. He got all of us guys from the mess hall together around a huge pile of potatoes and passed out peelers. "Don't you say we never gave you a potato peeler," he grinned. So we all talked and peeled potatoes that day. It was fun.

Our other mess sergeant, Dale F. Meyers, was set to be discharged at almost the same time as me. Dale was the one who handed me the piece of shrapnel that went through my headboard, back when I returned from my vacation in Da Nang. Normally we couldn't sit together at meals since we were of different ranks, but in those last days we sat together anyway and talked about what we'd do when we got home. "We could pay cash for motorcycles and drive them around the United States," he said one day. I thought that sounded like a grand idea.

On September 2, Master Sergeant Sanders signed my release orders to go back to the States. My ticket home was my manifest to get on the plane.

Master Sergeant Sanders signed it and handed it over to me. He smiled. "Good luck," he said.

I shook his hand. "Thank you so much, sir," I replied, smiling back.

Over the next few days, I turned in all my gear to the supply depot, including my M16 rifle. I took my leave of everyone in the mess hall for the last time.

"Thank you, guys. Nice working with you," I told them.

Then, early on the morning of September 9, a jeep drove me to Da Nang Air Force Base, and I boarded the Capital Airlines flight that would take me and ninety other soldiers home.

I had mixed emotions as I got on that flight. On the one hand, I was overjoyed to be leaving. At the same time, I could hardly believe it was happening. The thirteen months I'd spent in that country felt like an entire lifetime. The reality that I was actually leaving was unbelievable. I felt like I was dreaming.

The plane taxied down the runway and lifted into the air. When we were some ways off the ground, it banked to the left. I looked out the window that I was sitting by at the red clay down there on the ground below, stretching away from me.

Goodbye and good riddance to that Godforsaken place, I thought. *War is hell on earth. Vietnam is hell on earth.*

I hope I never come back here again.

ESCONDIDO, CALIFORNIA

Photograph of PFC Paul W. Simmons next to a purple cross
created by Marco Williams and Gary Nichols.

August, 2015

Chapter 9

HOMECOMING

*If you confess with your mouth
the Lord Jesus, and believe in your heart
that God has raised him from the dead,
you will be saved.*

—ROMANS 10:9

Prayers change things. For us, they sure did. My faith was strong, and I always believed that God would bring me back alive.

That fourteen-hour flight from Vietnam to Anchorage, Alaska, felt a little surreal. We made just one stop in Japan for an hour or two to refuel, and then we were on our way again. The three airline attendants on the flight seemed like angels in their blue uniforms, with their blond hair combed into smooth buns at the bases of their necks. They were beautiful, and we were very quiet and grateful as they served us on the plane.

We landed in Anchorage around midmorning on September 10, 1970. Our layover there lasted just a few hours while they gave us our shots—about eight of them altogether. My arm was sore for days afterward. Then we filed back onto the plane and flew farther south, to Seattle, Washington.

Even though I was officially discharged on September 10, it took another day for my papers to come through. I stayed in Seattle overnight, and that was where I got my first real taste of being back in the States. They gave us a hot shower followed by a free steak dinner, complete with a baked potato, chives, and sour cream. We slept in the barracks at Fort Lewis, and compared to the makeshift wooden buildings and mosquito nets of Vietnam, those brick walls and clean, comfortable beds felt like luxuries. It wasn't hot and humid anymore. Best of all, there weren't any rockets coming down.

That first day back, for the first time in over a year, I slept well. I called my parents and told them that I'd be heading home in a day or two, as soon as my discharge papers came through.

Then, on September 11, 1970, that day came.

The U.S. Army released me with an honorable discharge. They handed me my papers, along with $1,000 cash in discharge pay. And that was it. I was on my own again, free to go back to civilian life. For the first time in almost two years, I didn't have to take orders from someone of higher rank. I could make my own way and do what I wanted to do. An enormous weight lifted off my shoulders.

I was elated. Finally, my life belonged to me again.

The first thing I did was fly back to California to see my family. When I arrived at Los Angeles International Airport, I hailed a cab and made the twenty-minute drive home, watching the familiar landscape go by outside the window.

Then the taxi pulled up to the house.

It wasn't a big house. There was nothing special about it compared to the rest of the neighborhood. It had sage green walls and a gray-and-white-shingled roof. Out front was the simple brown fence I'd built for my mother with my own hands. That little building was small, but it held my whole life, growing up. It was home sweet home.

I got out of the cab and looked up. There, spread across a third of the roof, was a white bedsheet with three huge, OD-green words painted on it in capital letters:

WELCOME HOME PAUL!

That was the moment when my homecoming became real to me.

A minute later, I would pay the taxi driver and walk up the pebbled driveway into the house. I would embrace my parents and my brother, Jim, and the four of us would sit down to a delicious meatloaf dinner fixed especially for me. Another two weeks would see me on the road in the new VW Bug I would purchase with my wages from the war, crossing the green corn belt of Iowa on the adventure around the country that Sergeant Meyers and I had dreamed about. Eventually, I would return to California, where I would ultimately meet my wife, Alicia.

But in that one moment, standing on the road and looking at that sign, I knew that this—my homecoming—was really happening. I didn't have to pinch myself. I was looking at the answer to the prayer I'd first spoken on my knees in Vietnam: the prayer that

God would bring me home alive. Tears coursed down my face. I couldn't hold them back.

After seven miracles, God had brought me back safe from the war. I never forgot that. And I remain grateful to this day.

About the Author

Paul William Simmons was born in Torrance, California, in 1948. He served in the Vietnam War for thirteen months, from August 1969 to September 1970. He and his wife, Alicia, live in Escondido, California.